HIGH SCHOOL
the real deal

Juliana Farrell   Colleen Rush

From GPAs to Graduation

HarperTrophy®
An Imprint of HarperCollinsPublishers

For information address
HarperCollins Children's Books,
a division of HarperCollins Publishers,
1350 Avenue of the Americas, New York, NY 10019.

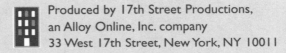

Produced by 17th Street Productions,
an Alloy Online, Inc. company
33 West 17th Street, New York, NY 10011

Library of Congress Cataloging-in-Publication Data
Farrell, Juliana
High school, the real deal : from GPAs to graduation/
by Juliana Farrell and Colleen Rush.
p. cm.
ISBN 0-380-81314-9 (pbk.)
1. High school students—United States—Juvenile literature. 2. High
school students—United States—Conduct of life—Juvenile literature.
3. Study skills—Juvenile literature. [1. High schools. 2. Schools.]
I. Rush, Colleen. II. Title.

LA229 .R87 2001
373.18—dc21   00-066219

First Avon edition, 2001

AVON TRADEMARK REG. U.S. PAT. OFF.
AND IN OTHER COUNTRIES,
MARCA REGISTRADA, HECHO EN U.S.A.

Visit us on the World Wide Web!
www.harperteen.com

Table of Contents

high school

survival
strategies

myths, tips, tricks, and more

You've heard all the horror stories;

you've seen all the movies—now it's time

for the real deal: high school. Is it really

as scary and intimidating as it's cracked

up to be? Nah. The fact is, high school is

whatever you want it to be. You can sulk

through high school with your head

buried in your book bag or you can blaze

a different path and make the most of

the next four years of your life. So

what's it going to be?

Top-Five Myths about High School

The first rule of thumb when it comes to high school? Don't believe everything you hear. From ghost stories to gossip, half of the stuff that's whispered in those hallowed halls is pure fiction. Check out these common high school myths.

myth: High school teachers are ogres.

truth: Teachers are human. They have good and bad days, just like the rest of us. But believe it or not, they're there to help you, not to make your life miserable.

myth: Upperclassmen hate freshmen.

truth: Every single upperclassman was in your shoes once upon a time, so they can sympathize...to a point. Okay, so there might be a couple of bad apples in the senior class who have been waiting three long years for their turn to trip up freshmen. But generally seniors have got much more than you on their minds (think colleges and careers).

6

myth: You'll be buried in homework.

truth: You'll have a bigger workload and teachers do expect more out of you, but you'll see the light of day every now and then. And most of the time, if you're knee-deep in papers and homework, teachers will cut you some slack if you let 'em know you're over-loaded (just don't expect to get away with this very often).

myth: It's best to just blend in.

truth: If you try to get lost in the crowd, you will. Being anonymous won't make high school any easier—just a lot lonelier. Even if you're shy, it's better to be noticed than to be wallpaper.

myth: Freshman year sucks.

truth: Your freshman year will be full of ups and downs. Some days will suck; other days will rule. But this roller-coaster ride is all part of learning about who you are and what you want out of life. So, enjoy it while it lasts.

The Dos

AND Don'ts

for your first day

(and Beyond)

They say high school is the best four years of your life. So why do those two words make you feel like there's a two-headed monster doing back flips in your belly? Because you're new at it. Remember middle school? Your spanking new clothes and school supplies couldn't hide the fact that you were a nervous puddle of sweat and flesh that first day. But you survived it, like everyone else. Still need help? Here are few hints on how to ace your first day.

do memorize your schedule. While you're at it, figure out which of your friends are in your classes. It might seem geeky, but being a bit overprepared beats walking into the wrong class any day.

don't be intimidated. Think about it this way: It's the first day for at least one-fourth of the student body, and they're just as lost, scared, and clueless as you are. So act confident (even if your insides are quivering like Jell-O).

do ask for help, directions, and advice. Nobody's going to call the freshman police if you fess up to being confused. Most people are more than willing to dole out words of wisdom, whether it's the lowdown on a teacher's pet peeves or how to navigate the lunch line.

don't beat yourself up when things don't go your way. So you fell for the ol' fifth-floor-swimming-pool scam, or you did a face plant in front of the entire football team. Big deal. You can stew in your mistakes and be miserable, or you can laugh at yourself (uh, along with the rest of the school) and bounce back after you've finished blushing.

do get involved. Some schools host an orientation fair or club day, and you can sign up for tons of extracurricular activities—from sports teams and spirit groups to student government and foreign language clubs. In the immortal words of a sneaker company, just do it. As cliché as it sounds, joining a club is the best way to meet new people. Besides, you'll need more than a killer GPA on your résumé when it's college application time.

don't overcommit yourself. It takes a while to get used to a new schedule, a new school, and, basically, a whole new way of life, so don't sign up for every club that piques your curiosity. Pick one or two activities that you're into and stick with 'em. Once you get the hang of high school life, you can always take on more.

do get enough sleep, eat right, and exercise. Sure, it's common sense, but when you're worked up about your first day or your first exam, snoozing, snacking, and doing Tae-Bo are pretty much the last things on your mind. But the truth is, all of those things can soothe you when you're stressing and give you the energy and brainpower you need to do your best.

don't try to be someone you're not. Sometimes it's hard to be original when everyone else is wearing the same style and has the same haircut, but cloning is for sheep, not people. Nothing says "lacks self-confidence" louder than trying to fake who you are. So you're not a fashion diva or a sports jock, or maybe you'd rather hang out at a museum than at the mall. Be yourself, no matter what. That means speaking your mind and standing up for yourself (and others) even if your attitude or ideas aren't popular.

do read the student handbook. Whether you're curious about the dress code or want to find out the school's policy on harassment, it's in there, along with all the rules of the school, maps of the campus, phone numbers, and, most important, a list of vacation days.

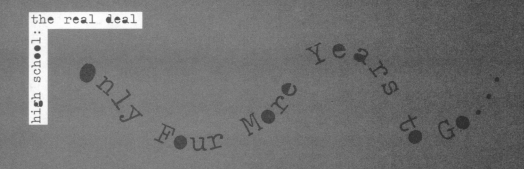

Only Four More Years to Go...

You came, you saw, you conquered your first day of school. Now what about the remaining 719 days? Here's the abbreviated version of what you can expect from the next four years of your life—the good, the bad, and the ugly.

Freshman Year

the good: You know that saying, Today is the first day of the rest of your life? Well, that's how you should look at your freshman year. You're starting all over again with a squeaky-clean slate. Maybe your grades weren't great in junior high, maybe you were hanging out with the wrong people, or maybe you were the model student. Whatever your pre-high school history, freshman year is your chance to turn yourself around or keep yourself on track.

Another first-year bonus? Making mistakes is practically a requirement for freshmen. Everyone knows you're new and expects you to goof up—a lot. Getting lost on the way to English lit, erasing entire research papers on your computer, falling down three flights of stairs—it's all part of the "learning process" (in other words, you learn what not to do and laugh it off in the end).

the bad: Is everything in high school gigantic, or is it just you? Call it the gnome syndrome or the dwarf complex, but high school can seem huge during those first few months. Big books, big classes, big assignments, big tests, big people—even the lockers are larger than life. Although school might seem like some kind of freakish Alice-in-Wonderland world, the reality is, it's not. It's kind of like when you sat on Santa's lap for a picture when you were a tyke. The jolly one looked enormous back then, but nowadays he doesn't seem so impressive. The same goes for everything in school. Once you're more comfortable with your surroundings, they won't seem so intimidating.

the ugly: No matter how you slice it, you're still the lowest form of life on the high school food chain. Don't take it personally. Torturing freshmen is a tradition that just won't die. People might call you dumb names, like "frosh" or "fresh meat," or try to trip you up because, well, they have too much time on their hands. Fortunately, most of the time the jokes and the name-calling are just harmless ways of teasing the new kid on the block. Unfortunately, there are people who thrive on making others miserable. These bullies aren't on the playground anymore. They've graduated to picking on freshmen and anyone else they think they can push around, but you can push back. You don't need to start a slugfest, but you should stand up to anyone who hurts you. Whether you confide in a teacher, the school counselor, or even your parents, it's your job to let someone know what's going on so it doesn't happen to anyone else.

Sophomore Year

the good: You're not a freshman anymore! There's a whole new class of confused students bumbling around, so your first-year jitters are over. You'll be more comfortable with the school routine and understand more about what's expected of you as a student. This is also the time to get more involved with activities that give you a sense of satisfaction and accomplishment. Being active, whether you're playing football or running for sophomore-class president, helps you realize your goals and gives you a better feel for what your future has in store. Best of all, you'll have more freedom. Without the freshman stress of fitting in and keeping up and the upperclassman pressure to deal with college applications and SATs, you've got plenty of time to do your thing.

the bad: Freedom comes with responsibility, and you can count on people—particularly teachers—to expect a little more out of you. Your classes will be a little harder, your assignments a little longer, and your workload a little heavier because your teachers know you've adjusted to the demands of a high school schedule. The key to keeping up? Get organized, learn how to manage your time, stay motivated, and ask for help whenever you need it.

the ugly: You're hanging in limbo land. Everyone is looking out for the freshman class while they make the tough transition from junior high. At the same time all eyes are on the upperclassmen as they write college essays and cram for entrance exams. That leaves you somewhere in the middle, maybe feeling like the forgotten student. It's easy to get lazy because you're not focusing on life beyond high school (yet), but dropping the ball your sophomore year can set you up for some bad habits later on.

Junior Year

the good: Welcome to upperclassman status. Juniors are so close to ruling the school, they can taste it. This is the year that really counts when it comes to your transcripts and taking advantage of all the extracurricular opportunities at your school. You'll be as busy as ever, juggling classes, studying for entrance exams, and taking on more leadership responsibilities, not to mention keeping up with a booming social calendar (think homecoming, pep rallies, the prom, and more).

the bad: This is when the real pressure starts in. Although there's still time to turn your grades around if your GPA isn't all that, it takes more work and determination than ever. The real dilemma? Feeling torn between having fun and enjoying your new school status and getting serious and planning for life after college. Balance is essential. In other words, don't blow all your hard work because your days in high school are numbered, but don't take your future so seriously that you miss out on what makes high school so much fun.

the ugly: Between PSATs, ACTs, the SAT, and worrying about your GPA, you might want to go AWOL before the year is out. Everyone's asking where you want to go to college and what you want to major in, and you might not even know if you want to go to college. It's a good idea to talk to your parents or a guidance counselor about your options and start the year with a special calendar marked with important test dates, prep classes, and deadlines.

Senior Year

the good: (As if this needs any explanation.) Seniors are the BSOC (big students on campus), and there's no denying their power, influence, or sheer coolness. There's an unspoken bond between you and your fellow classmates because, while you're celebrating your last year in high school, you're also pondering the big question mark—your future. Everyone—including you—is interested in what you're doing, where you're going, and how you're getting there. Fortunately, you're more confident with who you are as a person (a far cry from your freshman days), so you can (and will) figure it all out somehow. Last but not least, it's time to enjoy the fruits of all your hard work and take advantage of fourth-year perks, like senior trips, class picnics, skip days, and the prom.

the bad: Senioritis usually kicks in at the beginning of your second semester, right about the time when all of your applications are in and your plans for life after high school begin to fall in to place. Part of you can't wait to get out of school and away from home, but another side is petrified about the new life you're starting—being a freshman all over again. Meanwhile, with your transcripts already sent to prospective schools, it's tempting to think that your GPA doesn't really matter anymore. Wrong. If you slack off your last semester, you run the risk of jeopardizing your acceptance into your top colleges, not to mention letting down your teachers, parents, and anyone else who helped you out along the way. It's important to stay focused and remember what all your hard work was for.

the ugly: Indecision, fear of the unknown, future panic—it's all part of being a senior. Now that everyone wants to know your plans, you actually need a plan. You'll take the SATs for the last time; you'll whittle down your list of colleges and explore any noncollege options that might interest you. It's crunch time, and you'll have to write essays and résumés, fill out applications, and meet deadlines, all while managing your usual school routine. The good news is, all of your planning and anticipation will pay off in the long run. You're working toward a final, inevitable goal: graduation.

QUIZ:
Are You Stress-Savvy?

Find out if you know how to handle life when things get hot.

Answer true or false to the following questions:

1. When you're stressed and studying, munching on healthy snacks, such as an apple, granola bar, or yogurt, will ease your mind.

2. The amount of sleep you get does not affect your stress level.

3. Cutting out caffeine and upping your exercise routine during tense times will minimize your stress.

4. Stress can be caused by anything—cramming for exams, parents pushing your buttons, or even falling for the cute guy or girl in your Latin class.

5. All stress is bad.

6. Procrastinating helps keep stress under control.

7. Taking slow, deep breaths when an anxiety attack is approaching helps to relieve the stress.

Scoring:

1. True. It's a fact that foods full of complex carbohydrates, such as pastas, breads, and fruit, can up your supply of serotonin (a feel-good chemical in your brain). When your serotonin level increases, you'll feel more mellow and your over anxious attitude will be at ease.

2. False. You snooze, you lose—it's no secret that skipping out on sleep is bad for your health, particularly when you're stressed and need the rest to rejuvenate your brain. Sleeping is like fuel for your body—without it, your ability to concentrate and deal with life's ups and downs diminishes. Unfortunately, stress can really take a toll on your bedtime habits, so make an extra effort to get enough Zzzzs when you're in the stress zone.

3. True. Caffeine can make you even more anxious than you already are, so ditching your double latte routine will definitely improve your mood when you're stressed. Exercise is also a proven angst-buster; when your heart is pumping, your body releases a chemical called adrenaline, which increases your heart rate and blood pressure and energizes your body and brain so you can deal with stress better.

4. True. There are no limits to the number of things that can cause stress—basically, anything that causes you to feel excitement or anxiety can be stressful.

5. False. There is such a thing as good stress—it's the thing that motivates your mind and pushes you to do things you might not ordinarily do, such as testing your running skills in a marathon or asking someone you like out on a date. No matter how you slice it, new experiences can be nerve-racking, but it's that little bit of anxiety that nudges you to do your best.

6. False. Putting off until tomorrow what you should do today is the sure way to stress city. Working under pressure makes an already angst-inducing task even more stressful because you're racing against time. Whether you're studying, writing a paper, or preparing for a speech, you'll feel rushed to finish your work, and chances are you won't do as well—two things guaranteed to up your stress level.

7. True. Taking deep breaths brings more oxygen into your body, which is an instant way to relax and reduce stress. When you're feeling anxious, stop whatever you're doing and close your eyes. Then, take ten slow, deep breaths, and think about solutions to your stress. Chances are, you'll feel 100 percent better by the time you're finished counting.

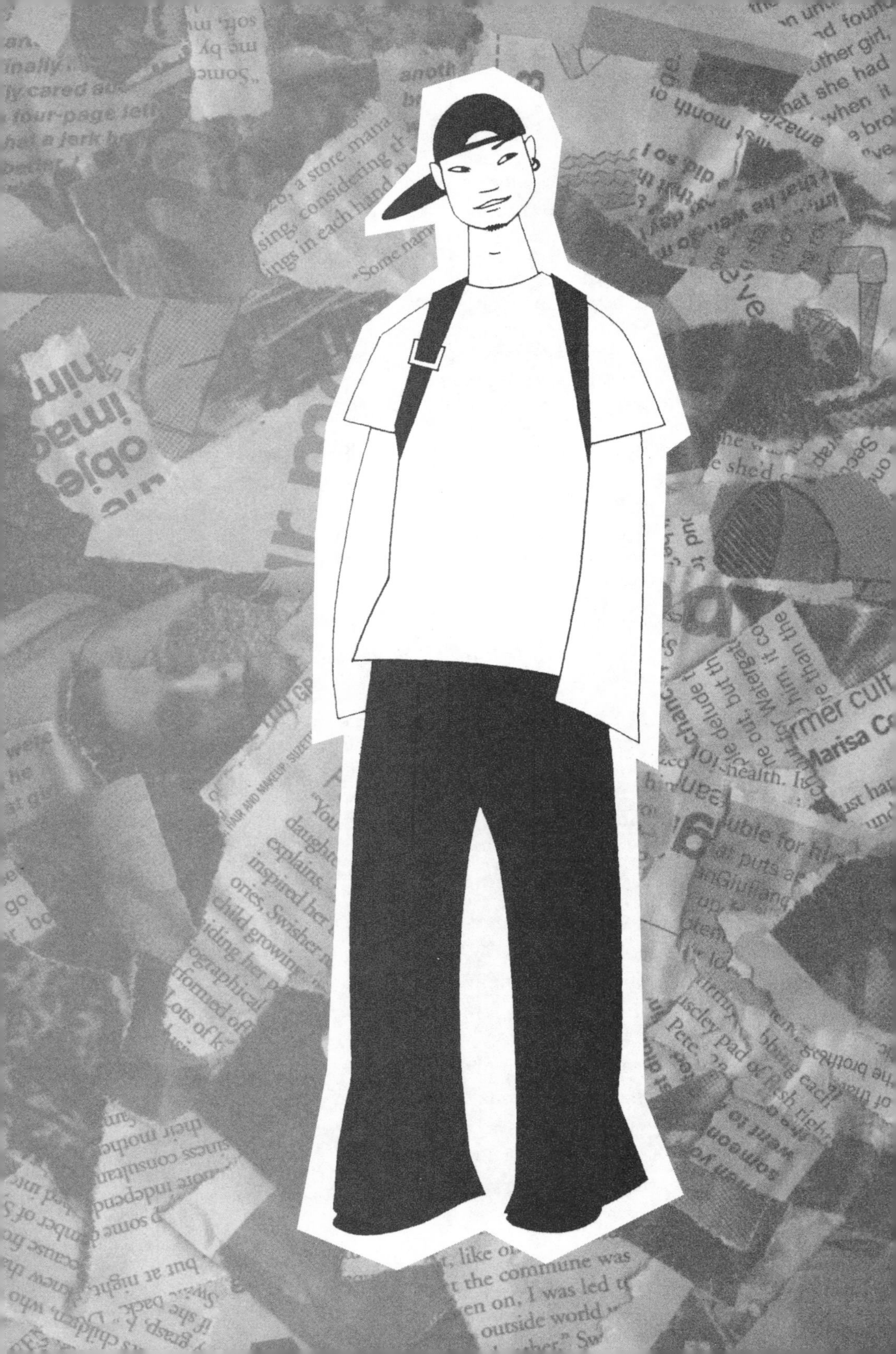

work, work, and more work:

high school
academics

Remember when your middle

school teachers told you exactly what

was going to be on a test and even gave

you a nice study guide to memorize?

Those days are over. Welcome to the

world of independent learning, where

teachers actually expect you to take

your own notes (ugh!), complete daily

homework assignments (gasp!), and

study. Want to know more? Read on.

What's So Different About High School Classes?

Well, for starters, you've got anywhere from five to eight different teachers bombarding you with book loads of new information on a daily basis. One minute you're deep in the heart of American history, the next you're facedown in a Shakespearean sonnet. So, after a grueling day of trying to absorb everything you hear (oh, and don't forget about keeping legible notes), you've got to go home and do it all over again to prepare for the next day's downpour of information. Remember: You have more than one class, and it's safe to assume that you'll have homework assignments in at least half of those classes. Is your head buzzing yet?

Is the Work Really Different?

In a word, yes. Up until now, most of the stuff you've learned is all about memorization—dates, spelling, multiplication tables, formulas, you name it, and you probably know the basics by now. Now that your head is stuffed with all the whos (Who was the twenty-third president?), whats (What is 132 divided by 12?), wheres (Where do adjectives go?), and whens (When did Columbus discover America?), you've got to figure out the hard part—the whys. This is a new level of thinking that goes way beyond memorizing, and it's tricky. There are opinions and theories, and best of all, there's not always a right answer to everything. Basically, you're learning how to think. That means you'll be analyzing authors, hypothesizing about scientific experiments, and more. Believe it or not, this is the fun part.

What's Up with the Pressure, All of a Sudden?

It might seem sudden, but you've spent the last eight years preparing for this. Sure, it doesn't seem like cut-and-paste time in kindergarten has much to do with freshman algebra, but all of your teachers along the way have been getting you ready for high school. By the same token, the tough classes, crazy workload, and high expectations your teachers have for you is preparing you for college or wherever you go after graduation. But what you learn goes beyond books. Teaching you to question ideas (why, why, why?) and search for the answers by yourself is one of the most valuable lessons of independent learning because it shows you how to trust—and rely on—yourself.

What Is Independent Learning?

In a nutshell, independent learning is all about knowing and doing what you're supposed to do without having anyone tell you what to do. It's kind of like your parents expecting you to keep your room clean without having to nag you about it. Ultimately, you are the only person responsible for yourself, your work, and your future, whether or not someone's there to help you along the way. Teachers aren't going to hold your hand while you research and write a paper for their class, and they won't keep reminding you when an assignment is due. Most of the time, teachers hand out a syllabus (an outline of assignments, exams, and deadlines) at the beginning of the year, and you're expected to keep up with it, whether or not they're keeping tabs on you. In other words, you're on your own.

still not clear what all of this means?

Here are some scenarios outlining what your teachers want from you. You'll have to:

- **Keep up with day-to-day and long-term assignments at the same time.** Example: You have a history quiz tomorrow, but you should also be working on the Civil War essay that's due in two weeks.

- **Know how to research.** Example: If you're writing an essay on Amelia Earhart, you'll need more than an encyclopedia. Do you know where to go or how to find the information you need? (Hint: Think library, the Internet, or even the video store.)

- **Take notes.** Example: During lectures, teachers can talk a mile a minute, so you won't be able to write down everything. As you listen to the lecture, you have to write down the information that's most important (that is, the highlights).

- **Study at your own pace.** Example: Some people can absorb three hundred years' worth of world history in thirty minutes. Other people aren't so lucky. You have to figure out how much time you need to spend studying per subject to stay on top of things.

- **Do all of your reading!** Example: You're supposed to read *Jane Eyre*, but your teacher didn't give you any questions or follow-up assignments on the book. That doesn't mean you won't be asked to summarize the book in a class discussion or take a pop quiz on it in two weeks.

- Ask for help when you need it. Example: You understand geometry like a fish understands legs—not at all. At some point (preferably before you've failed the class) you've got to let your teacher know that you need more help. You might have to stay after school for tutoring or take home extra work, but at least you'll pass. Otherwise your teacher will never know you're struggling . . . until it's too late.

- Set goals for yourself. Example: Keep a list of things you want to do in your life, from climbing Mount Everest to teaching kids to read. Whether it's a long-term goal (becoming an astronaut) or short-term goal (setting a track record), seeing your dreams on paper will help you stay focused on accomplishing them.

- Discover (and overcome) your weak spots. Example: You completely bombed a test. Is it because you didn't study long enough? Were your notes incomplete? Or did you have difficulty understanding the material? When you fail, don't think you failed because you're dumb. Think about what kept you from acing an exam and fix it, whether it means studying for another hour or borrowing notes from a friend.

- Manage your time. Example: You're in the school play, but you also have a paper to write and a book to read, and you're supposed to clean your room and wash the family car. You have to prioritize: How much time do you need to get each "job" done right? If you have trouble scheduling your time or remembering everything you have to do, invest in a day planner or pocket calendar.

GETTING your class act TOGETHER

Let's be honest: Studying in high school is no picnic. Not only do you have more classes and homework; the stuff you're studying isn't always interesting. But keeping up with your class time isn't rocket science, either. The secret to success is simple: Get organized, build your study skills, and ask for help when you need it. Read on for the straight scoop on how to do it all (and still have time for a life outside of school).

QUIZ:
Are You Notebook Neat?

Find out if your notebook skills pass the test.

1. Do you separate your old history tests from your geometry handouts?

2. Do you keep old class notes, exams, and quizzes handy?

3. Can you find class notes from a particular day or chapter?

4. Do you usually know when assignments are due?

5. Can you identify each notebook and which class it's for at a glance?

If you answered yes to most of these questions, give yourself a star. But if you need a little help staying organized, check out these notebook no-nos and other tips on how to keep your school life in order.

- Don't try to cram every subject into one binder or spiral notebook. Keep a separate notebook for each subject. If you want to keep more than one subject in a binder, group the classes by when you have them (that is, morning classes in one notebook, afternoon classes in another).

- Make sure each notebook has pockets (or use a separate folder) to hold loose work sheets, study guides, and homework.

- Color code your classes so you can tell each notebook apart at a glance.

- Date and write down any important information, like chapters or titles, at the top of the first page of new notes.

- Date and label all homework assignments and handouts.

- If you have a syllabus for each class, staple or paste a copy to the inside cover of your notebook for easy reference.

Homework Helper

Surprises should come in boxes wrapped in ribbon and pretty paper—not when you walk into the classroom. In other words, don't forget to keep track of your assignments and test dates, because your teacher won't always remind you. To do that, you'll need a day planner or calendar to pencil in due dates, homework, and other deadlines. Your homework planner should:

• Fit your lifestyle. Whether you're always on the go or "slow" is your speed of choice, your homework planner needs to suit your style. Some people keep track of their work in a mini-spiral notebook; others need a complete calendar—you need to figure out what works best for you.

• Be compact and easy to carry but big enough to fit all of your assignments, you'll need to bring the planner to every class.

• Have a space for dates and specific instructions for each assignment.

• Be easy to read. You should be able to figure out what's due (and what's done!) at a glance.

• Have a future. Be sure there's room to write down long-term deadlines (like midterm tests or final papers that are due in a few months).

The "S" Word: STUDYING

Just the word "study" is enough to make most people cringe, but it's a fact of life—if you want to make the grade, you have to study. The problem is, you aren't born with study skills. You have to learn how to study and, since everyone learns differently, figure out what study methods work best for you.

Five Study Techniques

1. Recopy your notes. Unless your brain is like a tape recorder, your lecture notes are probably going to be a little scattered, messy, and incomplete because you have to listen to your teacher ramble, figure out what's important, and write it down—all at once. Recopying your notes and filling in missing information or incomplete thoughts will help you review and relearn the material.

2. Reread and highlight. Pore over all assigned chapters and notes, highlighting important definitions, dates or theories, or any material you don't understand. Tests usually cover more than just a week's worth of material, so you have to backtrack and review the information that's not so fresh in your memory.

3. Flash cards. On index cards, write down blurbs of information you have to remember, like definitions. You can turn memorizing into a game and quiz yourself—or have your parents or friends quiz you à la *Jeopardy*—until you know the answers by heart. Shuffle the cards to keep them in random order, and carry them everywhere you go to review during downtime (like in line at the grocery store or waiting for the bus).

4. Study groups. It's a well-known fact that two brains are better than one when it comes to studying. If you have a study buddy or even a group of people to work with, you're more likely to understand the material you're studying. Not only can you quiz each other, but you can also answer each other's questions when your teacher isn't around to help you. If you're lost or just plain lacking good study skills, group study sessions will show you how other people work and learn and may show you that you're not alone in your confusion. But beware: Study groups can turn into gabfests if you're working with friends. You have to be strict about when it's time to study and when it's okay to slack off.

5. Memorize. There are lots of ways to memorize big blocks of material, whether you're trying to remember dates, names, formulas, or foreign words. Here are a few tricks:

Visualize. If you have a vivid imagination, visualize whatever you're trying to remember in a familiar setting. For example, if you need to memorize the first five presidents of the United States, look at a picture of each president and imagine them hanging out in your room. George Washington is watching TV, John Adams jams out to your favorite CD, Thomas Jefferson is wearing your pajamas, James Madison is making your bed, and James Monroe is reading your journal.

Rhyme. Make a poem out of the words or facts you have to remember. For example, if you're trying to remember key dates in early American history, think: Christopher Columbus set sail in 1492, but it wasn't until 1607 that the Jamestown colony grew; in 1620 the Pilgrims landed on Plymouth Rock, but in 1773 Bostonians had a tea party on the dock. The party led to the First Continental Congress in 1774, and by 1775 the Second Continental Congress was talking of war.

Acronyms and Acrostics. In acronyms, letters in a word stand for something else. For example, if you're memorizing the colors of the visible spectrum of light, think ROY G BIV: Red, Orange, Yellow, Green, Blue, Indigo, Violet. An acrostic is a made-up sentence in which the first letter of every word means something else. For example, if you're trying to remember the order of G-clef notes on sheet music, think Every Good Boy Deserves Fun (EGBDF). Sometimes the sillier the word or sentence, the easier it is to remember.

Chaining. If you have to remember a long list of words or ideas, make up a story that links the words together. For example, if you're trying to remember the periodic table of the elements, think: I'm going on a trip, and I plan to pack a hydrogen bomb, a helium balloon, lithium-flavored licorice, a drum of beryllium, boron in case I get bored, a carbon-dating machine (and so on).

HOW TO make studying LESS PAINFUL

Hitting the books doesn't have to be such a drag. Here's how to make your study sessions less painful and more productive.

- Study in twenty- or thirty-minute "bursts," and give your-self five-minute breaks in between. Stretch, get a drink of water, listen to your favorite tune, meditate—do anything that temporarily takes your mind off studying.

- Avoid distractions. It's difficult to concentrate on biology if your stereo is blaring or you're in the middle of a bustling coffeehouse. Find a quiet, comfortable place to study so you can focus on your work. Otherwise you'll spend twice as much time studying and probably remember half as much.

- Sleep, eat, and exercise. Nothing boosts your brain quite like a good night's sleep, nutritious food, and a little heart-pumping activity.

- Get into a routine. Whether you review your notes every night or wait until the weekend, get into a groove where studying becomes a habit (not a last-minute cram-a-thon).

- Reward yourself. When you finish a chapter or get ahead on your homework, give yourself a treat, whether it's that CD you've been dying to buy or a night watching totally mindless TV shows.

QUIZ: Do Your Study Skills Make the Grade?

Find out if your homework habits pass or fail.

1. The topic for your term paper is on the syllabus, which is given out the first day of class. You:
a) stuff the syllabus in your locker, and leave it there until the due date for the paper draws near—you work better under pressure.
b) outline a research and writing schedule, and figure out what you need to do each week so you're not left with a last-minute scramble.
c) spend all your spare time researching, writing, and editing the paper until it's Pulitzer-worthy.

2. Your typical school-night routine consists of:
a) cracking the books the second you get home, stopping only for dinner and bathroom breaks.
b) doing house chores and catching a little leisure-time activity (reading magazines, watching television, or gabbing on the phone) before you hit the books.
c) chatting online with your e-friends, catching up on your favorite TV shows, and avoiding your backpack like the plague.

3. When it's time to take notes in class, you:
a) date and title a new page in your notebook and listen for highlights of the lecture to scribble down.
b) prepare yourself for a nap because you've already schmoozed the best student in the class into letting you copy her notes.
c) start the tape recorder and whip out two pens (just in case one runs out), writing down each and every word your teacher utters.

4. You just realized the SATs are scheduled for the day after a killer concert you have tickets for. You:
a) scrap plans to see your favorite singer because you'll be studying 24–7 right up until the day of the test.
b) reschedule your test for a later date because this concert is a once-in-a-lifetime deal.
c) add a few more hours to your weekly study schedule so you can go to the concert guilt-free!

5. Your workload is out of control already, and you realize you have two term papers, a history test, and an art project due on the same day. Your nightly anxiety attacks are getting worse, so you:

a) buy a term paper on-line, "borrow" a sculpture from your artsy brother, and work on a foolproof crib sheet for the history test—there's no way you can pull off all that work by yourself.

b) kick up your coffee intake so you can stay awake and study longer.

c) schedule a meeting with each of your teachers to explain your dilemma, and ask for deadline extensions.

Scoring: 1) a=1, b=2, c=3; 2) a=3, b=2, c=1; 3) a=2, b=1, c=3; 4) a=3, b=1, c=2; 5) a=1, b=3, c=2

If you scored 12-15
BURNOUT BOUND. It's one thing to take school seriously, but sacrificing your social life for a flawless GPA won't make you a better student. At this rate, you'll crash and burn before the semester is over. The key to a killer high school career is finding a balance between work and play, because even the most stellar student needs a break from the books every now and then.

If you scored 9-11
CLASS ACT. Congrats! You've got this high school thing under control because you know how to strike a good balance between your hang-time and homework time. Lots of people think it's all or nothing when it comes to coping with high school, but you've found a way to make room for serious studying and take-it-easy leisures, which will make you a happier, healthier student in the long run.

If you scored 5-8
SCHOOL SKETCH. Wake up and smell the chalkboard—your lazy and lax attitude about school is endangering your future. You might think taking shortcuts and opting for the easy way out makes your life more manageable, but you're only cheating yourself when you put your schoolwork last. If you need help getting back on track, talk to a school guidance counselor about finding tutors and putting in after-school hours to make up for lost time.

Help: It's Not a Four-Letter Word

It's not always easy to admit that you might need help in school, but getting extra guidance, whether it's from a teacher or a tutor, doesn't mean you're dumb. It means you're smart enough to know you can't figure everything out on your own. So if you're lost in Latin or going crazy over calculus, here are three plans of action to help you get help.

Plan A: If you're struggling with a subject, talk to your teacher first. Explain what you don't get or why you're having trouble in the class. Be honest and open because your teacher needs to know where the problem is, whether it's because you can't see the board or because you're bored. Chances are, your teacher can help. You might have to change seats, do extra homework, or participate in after-school study sessions, so be prepared to do whatever it takes to get your grades back on track. But remember: Teachers are people. They're busy, and they've got hundreds of other students who might need help, too. If your teacher doesn't have the time or if the teacher is part of the reason you don't understand what's going on in class, there's always . . .

Plan B: Tutors. If you're stumped in one subject and the teacher can't give you the kind of attention you need, find a tutor who can help. Talk to the school guidance counselor about finding a free (or cheap) tutor from a community college or see if the National Honor Society at your school has a peer-tutoring program. There are also tutoring centers that might offer low-cost services. If all else fails, you might need to get a private tutor. This can be a bit pricey, but a private tutor can give you the one-on-one attention you need to succeed. If money is a consideration or the tutoring resources in your area are slim, try . . .

Plan C: Books, guides, the Internet, and more. Bookstores are stocked with study guides that make complicated lessons a lot easier. Some guides even have computer tutorials to give you more interactive tutoring sessions. In addition, the Internet offers limited on-line tutoring services.

A Close-up on Classes

Take a peek at your student handbook, and you'll realize that high school classes aren't the same old reading, writing, and arithmetic drill anymore. Although all schools have classes you're required to take in order to graduate, like English, history, and science, you'll also have a chance to choose "elective" classes that aren't required. Most schools have elective classes in every academic area (think creative writing/English, economics/social studies, statistics/math) so you can get a deeper understanding of your favorite subject. Other common electives are in the performing or visual arts, like band, chorus, art, theater, or dance, and in technical areas, like computers, wood shop, and home economics. Electives are usually more creative and fun than your required classes, but don't slack off just because it's a nonacademic subject. The grade you get counts the same as the grades for your regular classes.

You can count on your high school classes being a little harder and more time-consuming, but not impossible. You're basically building on what you learned in middle school, but your new classes will require more advanced thinking skills. Here's what you can expect from each of the major subjects you'll take:

English You can kiss book reports and summaries good-bye. High school English teachers don't want you to repeat information you've memorized; they want you to analyze it. Expect heavy-duty reading assignments (yes, that means reading entire books), writing projects, and class discussions. At this point you should be familiar with the basics of the English language, although you might have a class or two reviewing some of the ground rules of grammar. You'll have vocabulary tests, and you'll probably have to work on other communication skills, like speaking in public (think oral presentations).

Math

You'll be using all the algebra and pre-geometry skills you picked up in middle school, but high school math means pre-calculus, trigonometry, statistics, and more complex mathematical concepts. You need to know how to solve word problems and complete complex equations, and you'll have to keep up with the fast pace of the class. Follow the teacher's examples closely in class because you'll have to repeat the process in your homework and on tests.

Science

Labs make up a big part of high school science because you'll need to demonstrate hands-on knowledge of scientific theories. You'll also learn how to test the ideas that you form. And you'll incorporate some of your math skills in these classes and memorize lots of new terms—in addition to studying natural and chemical phenomena.

Social Studies

These classes cover a range of topics, from how the government works to American history. Expect a lot of independent reading, class discussions, research papers, and oral presentations (along with memorizing historically significant events). You'll also be analyzing and forming opinions about particular time periods, along with participating in historical re-creations, debates, and other interactive class projects.

World Languages

In the beginning, you'll be graded on things like vocabulary, pronunciation, and basic understanding of the language. As you progress in a language, your teacher might not let you speak English in class and might expect you to follow directions and participate in speaking activities in the language. In the higher language levels, you'll be expected to read books and give oral presentations in the language. Even if you're not a fan of learning a foreign language, it's best to stick with it while you're in high school, then take the SAT II. A high score on this test may exempt you from having to take a world language in college.

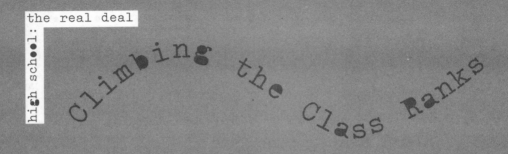

Climbing the Class Ranks

Wouldn't school be great if grades didn't matter? Well, stop day-dreaming. Grades do matter—right down to the peon scores on your pop quizzes. But in addition to your test scores and homework grades, your teacher has to weigh in on all aspects of your work, from your participation in class discussions to attendance. Somehow all of these factors boil down to one grade on your report card.

If you're interested in figuring out your average, keep track in your homework planner of every grade you get. Although there isn't one uniform grading scale, many schools go by the following one (or check your student handbook for your school's grading scale):

$$100-93 = A$$
$$92-85 = B$$
$$84-77 = C$$
$$76-70 = D$$
$$\text{Below } 69 = F$$

Teachers are usually required to calculate grades four to six times per year. If you're ever in doubt about how you're doing in a class, ask your teacher for your most recent average.

Your GPA (grade point average) is an average number that reflects all of your academic work. This is the number your school uses to rank you and it's the number colleges look at first. Class rank is listed from the highest GPA to the lowest. Calculating this average varies from school to school, but the following is a standard breakdown of how to translate each of your grades into a number value.

A = 4.0 points
A- = 3.7
B+ = 3.3
B = 3.0
B- = 2.7
C+ = 2.3
C = 2.0
C- = 1.7
D+ = 1.3
D = 1.0
F = 0

To calculate your GPA, add together all of your grades (using the number system above). Divide that number by the total number of grades you received, and you have your GPA. Here's an example:

1. Math: B+   (3.3 points)
2. Science: B   (3.0)
3. English: A-   (3.7)
4. History: C+   (2.3)
5. Spanish: B   (3.0)
6. Phys ed: A   (4.0)
7. Typing: B-   (2.7)
Total points: 22
Total number of grades: 7
GPA = total points (22)/total grades (7)
GPA = 3.1428571429

Keep in mind that every school calculates GPAs differently, so before you try to tally your GPA, consult your student handbook or ask your guidance counselor these questions:

• Does your school add only the final grade earned at the end of the course or the grade earned during each marking period?

• Does your school count physical education, health, and other elective classes in the GPA?

• Does your school give each class equal weight when adding the grades (even if some classes, like lab sciences, meet more often)?

• Does your school give weighted grades to students in honors, advanced placement, or other high-level classes?*

*Some schools calculate two different GPAs—one that values each class grade equally and one that is "weighted," or includes higher points for more difficult classes. For example, a "weighted" A in an advanced placement class might be equal to a 5.0 instead of a 4.0.

Does Your Rank Matter?

As if the pressure to get good grades and go to college isn't enough, all of a sudden you're supposed to worry about a tenth of a decimal point? Not really. Although colleges do look at your class rank and GPA, it's not the only determining factor in whether or not you get into a good college. Think about it this way: Hundreds of high school valedictorians with 4.0 GPAs apply to Harvard every year, and lots of them don't get in. Colleges are looking for well-rounded, interesting, and, yes, smart students—not just a number on a piece of paper. In other words, don't stress too much about your rank.

CLASS action

Because no two brains think alike, most high schools offer different levels of classes so students can learn at the right pace for them. Entrance into these levels might be determined by test scores, grades, a teacher recommendation, or even by the classes you took in middle school. Here's a breakdown of the basic levels and what they mean.

Advanced placement, or AP, classes are in essence college-level classes for high school students. These classes are typically offered to juniors and seniors, and they require a lot of reading and independent study. The best part? Most students who take AP classes take the AP test at the end of the school year. If your scores are high enough, you might qualify for college credits in a particular class. That means if you get a certain score on the math section of the exam, you can skip a math class in college, or you might qualify for a higher-level math course.*

Honors classes are usually offered for every academic subject in high school. These classes cover the same material as regular-level classes, but the tests, essays, and assignments are more challenging.

*See "Tests, Tests, and More Tests," page 56, on standardized testing, for more information about AP testing.

Regular-level classes offer students the standard level of education that's required by state law. The material you study and the tests you take are all on a level that students your age should be able to handle. Taking a regular-level class doesn't mean you're dumb or that you're stuck on that level forever. Everyone develops their academic abilities at different speeds, so you might start out taking regular-level classes and move up to honors or AP classes later.

Basic skills classes are designed to give students a solid base of information and skills that they missed in middle school. Again, taking these classes doesn't mean you're not smart or that you can't move into more challenging classes later. These classes are meant to help you catch up with other students your age and set the groundwork for regular-level classes.

Other schools have "tracking" programs that group students by their learning levels. The classes for each level, from high to average to low, are different. In other words, if you're on the high track, you might take biology your freshman year, but if you're in the average track, you might take earth sciences. However, it's not as easy to graduate from one track to another because you miss taking the initial classes of a higher track.

CH●●SING
classes

Yep, that's right. You get to pick and choose which classes you want to take. Sure, there are requirements that you have to fulfill, and you might not qualify for higher-level classes, but you do have a say in your class schedule. When you choose your classes, keep these tips in mind:

• Choose a level you're comfortable with. Classes should be challenging but not impossible. If you ever take a class that's completely overwhelming, chances are you're in the wrong level.

• When picking electives, don't follow your friends. Select classes that complement your skills. That's a tough call, especially if all of your friends are taking the same art class. But you have to go with your own gifts, whether it's playing the flute in band or taking a theater class.

• Pick classes that reflect your goals. Ideally, the classes you take should prepare you for your future. With that in mind, ask yourself these questions:

- Do I have the academic abilities (and interest) to get into a good college?

- Am I interested in getting a scholarship in athletics? Performance or visual arts?

- Do I want a career in a technical field, like computer programming or engineering, that doesn't require many liberal arts classes?

- Do I want to travel to a foreign country during high school or college?

- Do I need to make money while I'm in school to support myself?

Your answers to these questions can help you streamline your schedule so that you're taking classes that will help you achieve your goals. For example, if you want to travel around the world, taking Spanish or French classes will help you while you're globe-trotting.

So what if you're undecided about your future, or you don't know if you want to go to college? In spite of all the pressure to get the right grades, take the right tests, and get into the right school, going to college is not your only option. There are high school programs that will prepare you for whatever life after high school has in store. Ask your guidance counselor if your high school offers any of these non-traditional programs:

Vocational-technical, or vo-tech, schools offer classes that give students practical training in almost any career you can imagine, from landscaping and computers to fashion and design. Instead of listening to lectures or getting buried in book work, these classes are all about hands-on learning. Classrooms are equipped with gear to teach you the real skills you'll need to pursue a career.

Cooperative education programs offer students the opportunity to get real-life experience while they're still in school. Students spend half of the day in school and half of the day working at a real job. They not only get paid for their work, they also get school credit.

LEARNING
disabilities

Sometimes, no matter how much a person studies or what level of classes he or she takes, classes can seem overwhelming and impossible. It has nothing to do with a person's intelligence or motivation, but it may be a problem with how his or her brain processes information. Learning disabilities can affect people's ability to interpret what they see and hear or make it difficult to link information from different parts of the brain.

Having a learning disability doesn't mean you're dumb or slow. In fact, many people with learning disabilities have higher-than-average IQs. Leonardo da Vinci was dyslexic! In other words, learning disabilities don't have to hold you back. If you have difficulty in your classes, talk to your parents or a teacher you trust about getting tested for a learning disability. If you're diagnosed, you'll get an IEP (individualized education plan), which outlines ways that your school can help you succeed. You might be allowed to use a word processor in school or given extra time on tests. Some students simply need extra tutoring or textbooks on tape.

If you're diagnosed with a learning disability, try these classroom and study tips:

- Explain your learning differences and needs to all of your teachers.

- Sit at the front of the classroom.

- Review new vocabulary words with your parents, a friend, or a teacher.

- Borrow notes from your teacher or other students in your class.

Tests, Tests, AND MORE tests!

If death and taxes are the only certainty in life, tests are the only certainty in high school. Get used to the idea. National standardized tests are used to compare you with other students around the country. Some tests are state mandated, and you'll need to take them in order to graduate. Although you're not required to take some standardized tests, colleges use test results in deciding admissions. In other words, if you're planning to go to college, take the tests. Even if you're not college bound, it's not a bad idea to test just in case you change your mind. The tests can also help you determine where your strengths and weaknesses are and how you compare to students on a national level.

MAJOR standardized TESTS

Here's the scoop on the major standardized tests:

PSAT
(Preliminary Standard Achievement Test)

What is it? Just like it sounds, the PSAT is the pretest to the real SAT. The subjects and questions are similar to those found on the SAT.

Why should I take it? Besides giving you an idea of what it's like to take a standardized test, your scores reflect how you might do on the SAT as well. PSAT scores are also used to determine your standing for the National Merit Scholarship.

Who takes it? Some students take a "practice" PSAT during sophomore year to see what the test is all about and then take the test again junior year to improve their scores.

SAT I
(Scholastic Assessment Test)

What is it? The SAT I is a three-hour test that covers verbal and math skills. The verbal section covers vocabulary, reading comprehension, analogies and antonyms, and sentence completion problems. The math section requires knowledge of basic arithmetic, algebra, and geometry. The questions are intentionally tricky and confusing and are designed to determine what kind of thinker you are.

Why should I take it? If you're planning to go to college, most schools require you to take the SAT I and determine your admission status based on your test score.

Who takes it? Juniors and seniors. If you score low the first time you take the SAT I, you can take the test again. All of your scores will be reported to the colleges you select.

SAT II

What is it? The SAT II goes beyond verbal and math testing and focuses on specific subjects you've studied, like American history, biology, and French. Unlike the SAT I, these tests focus more on content and your basic understanding of a subject and not so much on how you think or reason. It's also shorter—only one hour per test.

Why should I take it? Many colleges require you to take a few SAT IIs, but it varies from school to school.

Who takes it? It's open to any student who wants to take it.

ACT
(American College Test Assessment)

What is it? The ACT is very similar to the SAT, although it tests your knowledge in four areas: English, math, reading, and science reasoning. The test is also administered six times per school year.

Why should I take it? Many colleges will accept your ACT scores in lieu of SAT scores. The test is also more common in western states.

Who takes it? Sophomores, juniors, and seniors.

AP Tests
(Advanced Placement Tests)

What is it? AP tests are usually given to students after they have completed a year of college-level, or AP, classes. However, if your school does not offer AP classes, you may still take the test. There are different exams for each subject, like art history or government and politics, and they usually consist of multiple-choice questions and essay sections.

Why should I take it? Many colleges will give you credit if you get a high score on an AP test. In the long run, that means you won't have to take the class again in college (yay!), and you'll have more space in your schedule to take a fun elective or a higher-level course in the same subject.

Who takes it? AP students or anyone who pays to take the test.

PREP SCHOOL

Preparing to take a standardized test can be a nightmare because you're not tested on one book or a single chapter. These tests cover everything you've learned so far, from subject-verb agreement to photosynthesis and everything in between, so forget about trying to cram before these exams. If you're gearing up to take a standardized test, here's what you have to do:

1. **Take a test prep class.** Princeton Review and Kaplan classes are the most well known of the bunch, although you may find less expensive, local classes in your area. These companies offer crash courses in all of the subjects you'll be tested in and are designed to review what you're already supposed to know. These classes will also shed some light on what it's actually like to take a standardized test, including sample questions from previous tests. Some of these classes are offered on-line as well. If you can't find a prep class locally or on-line, consider hiring a tutor who specializes in SAT preparation.

2. **Buy test prep books.** Bookstore shelves are piled with test prep books that include review chapters on important material and sample tests for you to take. Avoid gimmicky books that promise to raise your scores (or you get your money back!). Stick with books that offer lots of sample tests based on actual questions from past tests.

3. **Take practice tests.** Whether you find one on-line or in a book, you should take at least one full-length practice test to get a feel for the types of questions you'll be asked. If you plan ahead, take several sample tests and figure out which section or type of question you miss most often.

4. **Relax.** Although these tests are important, they're not worth losing your mind over. It's easy to get caught up in the competition and stress out about your scores, but all of that pressure won't help you on the big day. You have to take care of your body as well as your mind when you're preparing for these tests, so take deep breaths, get enough sleep, eat right, and exercise. Besides, even if you blow it, you can take most of these tests again.

how to fail IN HiGH school

Academic Crimes and Punishment

So, you want to fail? You're trying to get kicked out of school? Here are

three surefire ways to get the boot (or at least a big, fat F):

Cheating Crib notes scribbled on your shoe. Cheat sheets tucked in your shirt. Spying on your neighbor's test paper. Morse code answers tapped out on your desk with a pencil. Guess what? Your teachers have seen it all and then some. Students come up with some pretty creative ways to cheat, but the fact is, teachers are wise to those sneaky ways. They sense cheaters like tigers smell fear.

Plagiarism That's a big word that basically means you tried to take credit for something you didn't write. This is tricky business because you have to write papers and essays that require you to do research. You'll come across lots of brilliant, well-written material that says exactly what you want to say, and it's really tempting to borrow a clever line or two. But guess what? It's wrong. Unless you put quotes around that sentence and write a footnote about where you got the information, you're plagiarizing material that's been copyrighted. Big mistake. Oh yeah, it's against the law, too.

Copying A close cousin to plagiarism, copying goes something like this: You stayed up too late surfing the Net or gabbing on the phone, and you "forgot" to do your homework, so you borrow your best friend's homework and copy it. Bad idea. Not only will your teacher notice that you and your best friend got the same questions right and wrong (strike one), but you miss out on learning the assignment (strike two). Chances are, you'll be tested on whatever you copied (strike three). You're out!

More Academic No-Nos

Everyone bags their homework every now and then. Maybe the game went into overtime or you fell asleep before you finished your algebra problems. Maybe the shoe sale at the mall was more important than reading five chapters of *The Grapes of Wrath*. Or maybe you just didn't feel like writing an essay on Benjamin Franklin. Whatever the case, you flaked out on your work and you're fishing around for excuses to feed your teacher.

"My computer blew up!"

"My dog died!"

"I was kidnapped by aliens!"

Your teacher has heard everything. Even if she buys your lame excuse, it won't work the second time you slip up, whether or not you're telling the truth. The smart way to handle the situation? Tell your teacher you couldn't finish the assignment. If he or she asks why, tell the truth. Some teachers might give you an extension on an assignment, but others might drop your grade for every day that it's late. It all depends on the teacher, so be prepared to pay the price for slacking.

Chapter 3

GET A LIFE!

(at school)

Get up. Go to school. Go home.

Get up. Go to school. Go home. Get up. Go

to school. Go home. Get up. Go to school.

Go home. Get up. Go to school. Go home.

Get up. Go to school. Go home. Get up. Go

to school. Go home. Get up. Go to school.

Go home. Get up. Go to school. Go home.

Get up. Go to school. Go home. Get up. Go

to school. Go home.

TOP-SEVEN REASONS
to get a life

You could spend the next four years of your life in a boring routine, but why? High school is the prime time to discover your passions and develop your talents. Extracurricular activities, or any organized student club, team, or group that's active outside of the regular school day, aren't just extra padding for your résumé or college applications. In fact, getting involved outside of the classroom is a little bit like scoring an extra candy bar out of a vending machine. If you put a little bit into it, you get a lot more out of it.

1. Friends, friends, friends. If you're still hanging out with the same crowd you went to middle school with, don't you think it's time to branch out a little? Joining a club, team, or any other organization at your school is a 100-percent-guaranteed way to meet new, interesting people who dig the same things you do.

2. Discover hidden talents. You'll never know that you have a gift for pole vaulting, picketing for equal rights, or playing chess until you try. Maybe you've always wanted to go rock climbing, or maybe the Golf Channel fascinates you. Unless you explore the things that excite you, you'll never discover your natural abilities. Ask yourself, What do I like to do? What would I be doing if I didn't have to go to school or work? Chances are, you can find a club that fits whatever piques your curiosity.

3. Attract members of the opposite sex. Who says parties are the best places to meet people? The fact is, joining an organization gives you an instant icebreaker. You automatically share something in common with everyone in the club, which isn't always true with fiestas. And there's nothing more attractive to the opposite sex than someone who is involved, interesting, and has a life outside of school.

4. Boost your self-confidence. Nothing beats the satisfaction of being a leader and a team player. Getting involved in activities that don't revolve around numero uno makes you feel great about yourself, and that vibe is contagious. People will pick up on your I-can-do-it attitude and treat you with more respect. They'll value your opinions and advice, and you'll feel more comfortable going for other goals and getting active in the world. Even if you fail or figure out that you're not interested in a club, the fact that you still gave it a shot means you'll never have any regrets.

5. Blow off stress. After a long, hard day of brain-busting exams or mind-blowing class discussions, the very best way to unwind is to take your mind off school. Whether you're rehearsing with the theater club or training with the track team, focusing on an extracurricular activity and doing what you do best will help you forget a downer day and boost your mood.

6. Get an education in life. Street smarts, life skills, Real World 101—whatever you want to call it, the fact is, there are lessons in life that you won't learn about in books. Extracurricular activities take you out of the classroom and into reality. You see the world through other people's eyes, you learn to appreciate different perspectives, and you figure out how to deal with problems that no teacher could ever test you on.

7. Lure in colleges or potential career opportunities. You shouldn't join a club just because you think it'll look good on your college application or résumé, but the truth is, employers and admissions officers are more interested in active, involved people. School-sponsored clubs, organizations, and honors will show up on your transcript, and those activities say more about you than your report card. Joining extracurricular activities not only illustrates your talents and interests; it also proves you have go-for-it initiative and leadership skills.

Ready, Set, Go Get 'Em!:

high school

SPORTS

Team sports are probably the most popular extracurricular activities in high school. Even if you're not a jock, most schools offer a variety of sports at different levels of competition—from über-competitive football to ultimate Frisbee.

Intramural/Club Sports

Club sports are usually open to anyone who wants to learn the sport (read: no tryouts). Sometimes if a sport is new at a school (or if there are no nearby schools to compete in the sport), a school may offer the sport as an intramural or club sport to increase interest. For the most part, these sports aren't as competitive—the teams are more focused on learning the game and having fun.

Most schools have several teams representing each traditional sport (like football or basketball), but each team competes on a different level, and you have to go through tryouts to make a team.

Freshman Sports

Freshman sports are the training ground for players with a future. Their focus isn't necessarily on winning, because these teams are getting a crash course in high school sports—from learning the rules and regulations of a sport to getting to know coaches and clicking with teammates. It's also a chance for coaches to check your attitude and skills to see if you've got what it takes to compete.

Junior Varsity Sports

If you've got a good team-player attitude but not quite all of the skills to compete at the varsity level, JV teams offer players a chance to polish their game. Although some athletes might bypass this level, most athletes spend at least one year on a JV team to train for a shot at the big time: varsity.

Varsity Sports

Varsity games are the ones that pack the bleachers. Players have the maturity, skills, attitude, and competitive edge that make watching a sport as thrilling as playing the game. If you plan to get an athletic scholarship or play on the varsity level in college, getting a spot on your high school's varsity team is key.

What's your team type?

Are you into winning solo sports, or do you like to taste victory as part of a team? No matter what your team type, your school has a sport to suit your style.* But before you pick your game to play, ask yourself these questions:

• Do I like contact sports or non—contact sports?

• Do I like sports that rely on physical strength or a practiced skill (or both)?

• Do I care about the gender stereotype for a sport (e.g., girls aren't supposed to play football and guys shouldn't be cheerleaders)?

• Is the sport practical in terms of my lifestyle and environment (e.g., ice-skating in Arizona or snow skiing in Florida)?

• Can I handle the stereotype of the sport, if there is one?

Going-Solo Sports: Archery, bowling, cross-country running, equestrian, fencing, figure skating, golf, gymnastics, swimming, tennis, track, wrestling.

Team Games: Baseball, basketball, cheerleading, crew, football, hockey (ice and field), lacrosse, polo, rugby, soccer, softball, volleyball.

*If your school doesn't offer your sport of choice, start your own team! Read the student handbook or contact the sport's national organization for information about how to form your own intramural or club team.

JOIN the cluB!

School-sponsored clubs are limited only by your imagination. Whether you're rallying people for a protest or you just want to share your passion for cooking, chances are there's a club at your school that can make your dreams come true. Here's a look at a few of the clubs offered at most schools and how they fit into your future.

If you're interested in:	Club scene:
Government and politics	Junior State of America, Model Congress, Model United Nations, Mock Trial, student council, debate team, or speech club
Theater (acting, production, etc.)	Drama club, dramatic productions
Business and entrepreneurship	DECCA, Future Business Leaders of America, the student store
Music	Chorus, jazz band, marching band, orchestra, string ensemble
Journalism	School newspaper, television station, radio station
Activism	Environmental Action Club, Interact Club, Key Club, Students Against Drunk Driving, peer counseling
Writing	Student literary magazine, newspaper
Trivia	Academic Decathlon, Quiz Bowl team
Foreign language	Spanish, French, Latin, Italian clubs

members ONLY

In order to join most clubs, like many of those listed above, you simply need to sign up. Other organizations require an election, and participation is determined by student-body vote. But membership in some clubs, like the National Honor Society, is based on academic work, leadership skills, service, and character. These selective clubs stand out on high school transcripts because the faculty usually chooses the members, and the honor is a marker for well-rounded, quality students. If this sounds like a club you'd like to join, read your student handbook or talk to a faculty adviser about the requirements and standards for membership.

WAY to go!

Four no-brainer steps to extracurricular bliss:

1. Make a list of the clubs you want to join (or activities you enjoy). See your student handbook (or ask your guidance counselor) for a list of extracurricular activities.

2. Attend your school's activities fair, which showcases all the clubs, sports, and organizations, and meet people who belong to the groups you're interested in joining.

3. Sign up, try out, volunteer, or nominate yourself for your favorite extracurricular activities.

4. Commit to your club. Joining isn't just about being a name on the roster. Go to meetings, volunteer your time, and be an active, involved member.

Goal Getter

So you've set your sights on a sport or a seat on the student council. Now what? Unlike some activities, you can't just sign up to be a member—you have to work for what you want. That means getting on the bandwagon and running for office or mustering up the courage to audition in front of coaches and teammates. Scared yet? Auditions and elections aren't easy (if they were, everyone would be president!), but you will survive. Here's how:

- **Be prepared.** Whether you're giving a speech or showing off your running skills, get your act together before the big event. Write down notes, wash your lucky sweatband, psych yourself up—do whatever it takes to truly shine in your moment in the spotlight (or else the moment's shining, not you).

- **Don't sweat the competition.** Even if you think your fellow candidates or teammates are more qualified, don't get discouraged. Thinking negative thoughts will take you out of the game before it begins. By the same token, don't dis your competition. Dirty campaigns or trash talking during tryouts are not-so-wise ways to win enemies and lose supporters.

- **Rally for support.** Recruit your friends to help you train, cheer you on, or work on your campaign.

- **Practice.** Test out your speeches and audition by yourself before the big day arrives so you'll know your routine by heart.

- **Refuse to think like a reject.** Getting elected or being part of a team takes guts, determination, and a go-getter attitude. Even if you lose, you have to bounce back and be ready for more challenges. If you quit after your first try, you'll never have a second chance.

Extracurricular Etiquette:

The Dos AND Don'ts

Marisa Cohen

Do make time. If you join a club or team, be prepared to sacrifice some of your slack time for meetings, events, and fundraisers. Find out how much time each activity requires on a weekly and monthly basis. Does it fit into your schedule? Can you commit to regular attendance and involvement?

Don't overcommit yourself. Remember that thing called school? It's still important. If your extracurricular activities are biting into your class time, you might have to quit a club. Start small, then get more involved once you have a feel for your schedule.

Do talk to your teachers whenever an extracurricular commitment, like an away game or convention, means missing a class. Get all of your assignments beforehand, and keep up with the class no matter how many days you miss.

Don't be a flake. Whether you blew off a bake sale or forgot to ask your parents for a ride to an event, being a no-show more than a few times is worse than not belonging to a club at all. Buy a calendar to keep track of all of your commitments and give advance notice if you can't participate or if you need a ride.

QUIZ: Are You a Team-Player, or the Solo Type?

Find out what clubs and extracurricular activities suit your style.

1. When there's a job to do, whether it's collecting trash on a highway or petitioning to change school policy, you're most comfortable:
a) working quietly behind the scenes to make a difference.
b) at the head of the pack, rallying the troops into action.

2. If you wanted to start your own 'zine, you'd:
a) recruit a few of your closest friends to help you get it off the ground.
b) call a meeting of the student council to request funding and to organize the club.

3. Given the choice between writing a speech for the class president and running for class president, you'd choose:
a) writing the speech, because you express yourself better on paper than in person.
b) running for class president, because you have the ability to get people excited and interested in school politics.

4. If you had to set up a fund-raiser for your class trip to France, you'd:
a) suggest each student sell raffle tickets for an all-expense-paid dinner at a French restaurant.
b) suggest a classwide bake sale, with everyone cooking a different French dish.

5. You find out that your cafeteria is serving grapes picked by underpaid day laborers in a Third World country. To fight the injustice, you:
a) post protest flyers around school, then write to every member of the school board and your local congressman to bring their attention to the matter.
b) organize a massive protest rally before school, then contact the local news media to cover the event.

Scoring: Count the number of times you scored A or B.

If you scored mostly As, you're a

ONE-ON-ONE WONDER.

You know in your heart of hearts that one person can make a difference, so even though you're willing to work with others, you feel more at ease when you're solo. Getting the job done when you're on your own works with these extracurricular activities: newspaper and yearbook staff (photographer, writer, graphic designer), theater club (set and costume design), peer counseling, volunteer groups, solo sports (tennis swimming, track), literary clubs, tutor/mentor programs (Big Brother or Big Sister), or any do-it-yourself start-up clubs that cater to your individual interests (chess team, language club, etc.).

If you scored mostly Bs, you're a

MORE-THE-MERRIER MEMBER.

Being the center of attention and inspiring crowds is your calling in life. You're a natural-born leader with solid people skills. Getting involved with groups is easy if you join any of these school endeavors: student government or class-council officer, ROTC, debate team, marching band, activist groups such as Sierra Club or the Student Environmental Action Coalition, sports boosters, team sports (basketball, soccer, baseball, etc.), theater club (stage manager, director), and outreach volunteer programs such as Habitat for Humanity.

life 101

LESSONS YOU WON'T LEARN IN SCHOOL

If you're searching for some real-life experience while you're still in school, look no further. From flipping burgers to   filing   reports,   there's   a

part-time   job   out   there   with

your name on it.

TOP-FIVE REASONS TO GET A JOB

5. Stay out of trouble.

(What else can you do with all that spare time?)

4. Help out with family finances.

3. Earn dough for clothes, gadgets,

and other things your parents won't pay for.

2. Get real-world experience in your future field.

1. Save cash for college.

How to Get a Job

Money doesn't grow on trees, and neither do jobs. Scoring an after-school gig takes time and effort, but all your hard work will pay off when you cash that first paycheck. If you're ready to join the workforce, follow these steps to find the right job for you.

1. Make a list detailing the jobs you'd like to apply for. As you make the list, consider these questions:

- What do you want to get out of the job? Do you want a job that (a) pays well but gives you little career experience? (b) gives you loads of experience and networking potential? (c) offers a little bit of both?
- What are you not willing to do? (Although you might not have the luxury of being picky about your part-time job, rule out jobs that'll make you miserable.)
- How much time can you devote to the job?
- Do you have any previous job experience?
- What are your interests or hobbies? What jobs relate to those interests?

2. Prepare a résumé. Although most of the jobs you apply for right now might not require a résumé, it can't hurt to have one handy just in case. A résumé:

- Is no longer than one page.
- Should include your name, address, and other contact information.
- Outlines your previous jobs, skills, school achievements, awards, and interests.

3. Start the job hunt. When you're pounding the pavement in search of work, consider these resources:

- **Want ads** Check your local newspaper, the Internet, and community bulletin boards in coffee shops, bookstores, etc., for job listings.
- **Help Wanted signs** Scour Main Street, the mall, movie theaters, fast-food joints, and other high-school-friendly locations for job opportunities.
- **Friends and family** If someone you know owns, works for, or has contacts with a company you're interested in, ask about job opportunities. This can be awkward, so don't be pushy, and don't expect someone to get a job for you. Be genuine, let them know you're interested in their career, and ask for advice.
- **Cold calls** Based on your job wish list, locate several companies or businesses that you'd like to work for, then call 'em up or drop by for an informal introduction. (This shows your persistence and willingness to work hard to get what you want.) Talk to the manager or the person in charge of hiring. Here are a few questions to ask and points to bring up during the conversation:
  - Do you have any job openings right now, or will you have any in the near future?
  - May I leave my résumé and a job application with you to keep on file for future consideration?
  - I am interested in working for your company because (list reasons).
  - I think I would be a valuable employee because (list experience, etc.).
- **Volunteer** Sometimes the only thing standing between you and your dream job is money. If a company can't hire you as a part-time employee, whether it's because you're too young or they can't pay you, consider volunteering for the job as an unpaid intern. Working for free might not help you pay for a fab pair of shoes, but it shows potential employers that you've got character and determination.

4. Get references. You'll need to line up at least two people who can vouch for your skills and reliability, and your parents don't count. Think: former employers, teachers, a mentor, a coach, religious leaders, advisers, or friends of the family. Be sure to ask permission before you list them as references on your applications and résumé.

5. Apply for jobs. For some jobs, that simply means filling out a job application form. More competitive jobs might require a résumé (aren't you glad you did step 2 now?) and a cover letter. Complete the application requirements for each job, and double-check to be sure you've included everything, like letters of recommendation and work permits.

6. Interview. Even if you're applying for a job as a fry cook at a fast-food dive, show up for the interview on time and dressed professionally (read: no baseball hats, tank tops, or flip-flops). Your first face-to-face impression will last, and it can make or break your chances of getting a job. Interviews give an employer a chance to get to know you, so be prepared to answer questions about yourself, including

- Why do you want this job?
- Why should I hire you?
- What are your strengths/weaknesses?
- When are you available to work?

Interviews also give you the chance to ask questions.

- What are my job duties?
- Are the hours flexible?
- What is the company dress code?
- Is there a chance for promotion?
- What is the salary/pay scale?

89

7. Send thank-you notes to your interviewers.
This small gesture is not only polite; it also makes your name stand out when the time comes to hire someone. Remember: No job is too small for a thank-you.

8. Fill out work-related forms. Once you have a job, you'll need to fill out a work permit, which is required in most states for employees who are under 18. This permit lists your legal age and working status and tells your employers what they can and cannot expect from you according to state labor laws. You will also have to fill out an I-9 form, which establishes your eligibility to work, a W-4 federal tax form, and a state tax form. Ask your parents or a guidance counselor for help if you have questions about obtaining or filling out the forms.

9. Figure out your money matters. Now that you have a job, you have to decide what to do with your paycheck. (Hint: Blowing it all on video games isn't a good idea.) First, figure out how much you're making, then create a budget and stick to it. When you're dividing your dough into a budget, keep these questions in mind:

How much do you want/need to save per paycheck?

How much do you anticipate spending on clothing, entertainment, etc.?

How much do you need to save for taxes?

How much do you need to contribute to the family fund?

how to LOSE a job

Getting a job is hard, but keeping a job is the real challenge. Unless you're itching to get fired, don't

Show up late for work repeatedly.

Disobey safety regulations or company rules.

Ignore the company dress code.

Blow off schoolwork in favor of your job.

Call in sick frequently.

Forget to give adequate notice about days you cannot work (prom, SATs, family vacation, etc.).

how to QUIT a job

Chances are, you won't keep your part-time job forever. When quitting time comes, be sure to leave on a good note. You might need a letter of reference from your employer for a future job, or you might want your old job back at some point. Other quitting tips to remember:

Explain your reasons for quitting. Whether you're having a rough semester at school and need the free time to study or you got a better job offer, tell your employer exactly why you're quitting.

Give at least two weeks' notice before you quit so that your employer has time to hire someone to replace you.

Ask for a letter of reference. Unless you didn't get along with your boss, he or she will probably be happy to help you out. Most employers like to follow the career paths of their former employees.

If your reason for quitting is temporary, be sure your boss knows that you might want your job back at a later date. For example, if you take off two months for soccer season, tell your boss when you will be available to work again. You may or may not get the job back, but at least your boss will know you're interested.

community service WORK

If you truly want to learn some of life's most valuable lessons, be a volunteer. Participating in community service projects gives you all the perks of an extracurricular activity (see "Top-Seven Reasons to Get a Life," p. 68) plus bonus benefits, like the satisfaction of knowing you're helping others, working for a good cause, and making a difference in the world. Ask anyone who's ever volunteered and they'll all say the same thing: You get more out of it than you put into it.

The great thing about community service is that there are no limits to what you can do. Wherever someone is in need, whatever needs improving in your community, there's nothing stopping you from taking a do-it-yourself approach to the problem. For example, if you think a local park needs a makeover, why not raise money for the cause and organize a cleanup crew?

Getting involved is simply a matter of choosing a cause or finding an organization in your area that needs volunteers. Some of the more common community service organizations and activities include

- Hospitals

- Volunteer Ambulance Corps

- Crisis intervention and peer-counseling hot lines

- Tutoring

- Food banks and soup kitchens

- Nursing homes

- Homeless or battered women's shelters

- Fund-raisers

- Church outreach programs

Summer BREAK

If sitting on a couch and twiddling your thumbs all day long is your idea of a fulfilling summer, get a clue. Wasting those three free months of your life is like bingeing on a bag of potato chips: It might seem like a good idea at first, but in the end it leaves you feeling empty. Instead of watching TV and working on your tan this summer, check out these alternatives:

- Get a full-time job (see "How to Get a Job," page 87, for pointers).

- Go to summer school. Many universities offer academic summer programs for high school students.

- Go to camp. Whether you're into shooting hoops, riding horses, or reciting Shakespeare, there's a summer camp out there for you. Camps are also great places to meet people and sharpen your skills for the school year.

- Be a tourist. Broaden your horizons and get a new perspective on the world on family vacations, on road trips, or camping in the wilderness

Chapter 5

STRESS:
HOW TO HANDLE THE
pressures
OF HIGH SCHOOL

For some students, moving from middle school to high school is like going from zero to sixty miles per hour in two seconds. One day you're playing red rover on the playground at recess, the next you're speeding through classes, extracurricular activities, and home-work sessions, all while trying to make time for that thing called a social life and dealing with parents who don't seem to understand that you're growing up. It's enough to give you whiplash. But like everything else you're learning right now, the way you cope with stressful situations and the habits you form right now, as you get used to your life's new pace, will be with you forever. You can count on life serving up more madness once you leave high school, so now's the time to learn how to juggle all your responsibilities.

school STRESS

Picture it: Your friend needs your advice about a class. Your biology teacher expects you to make up a missed assignment after school. Your coach thinks you need to practice your backhand a little more. The debate team is scheduling a scrimmage with another school. Oh yeah—this is all going down on the same day. How would you deal? Think hiding out in your locker until next week seems like a reasonable answer? Think again. Remember, hiding won't be an option when you're in the real world. You need to fine-tune your coping skills. To help you along, here's a list of key words that'll make stress-management a lot easier.

Prioritize

Remember lining up for grade school photos according to height? That's what you have to do with your workload and school-related responsibilities. Mentally measure up each one of your commitments—from rehearsing for a play to studying for a test—and figure out what's tall (most important) and what's small (least important). Measuring, or prioritizing, your life is easiest when you have clear goals in mind. Do you want to graduate at the top of your class? Then academics are a priority. Do you want to get practical, real-world experience? Getting a job might be your priority. Do you want to pursue an athletic scholarship? Practicing to make the team might be your priority.

What if your goals aren't so crystal clear? You still have to prioritize your time. The trick is to adjust your priorities often—maybe even daily—and keep your options open. As you go along, you'll learn more about your strengths, weaknesses, and interests and figure out what your goals are. You should also get a better understanding of your work style and when you've reached your limit. All of these factors will influence your priorities and show you what you need to do to reach your maximum potential.

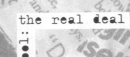

PITFALLS

of prioritizing

Don't let a parent, teacher, coach, or friend set your priorities for you. You know yourself best. Even if your dad thinks you need to play softball or your teacher wants you to go to medical school, it's ultimately up to you to decide your own fate.

Don't cling to goals that drain you. Chances are, if you're exhausted, frustrated, or burned out, you're spending too much time on something that's not a priority. Be flexible about your future and realize that you will change your mind—a lot. Readjust your schedule to suit your energy and interests.

Time Management: Once you've prioritized, you have to organize your schedule and make time for what's important. Here's a hint: Buy a calendar. Write down all the details of your schedule, from paper deadlines and exam dates to club meetings and after-school practices, and estimate how much time each activity will take. If you keep track of your time commitments, you'll have a better grasp on your goals, not to mention more time to unwind and do the things you like to do.

To-Do Lists: This one's a no-brainer. Listing your day-to-day duties serves as a visual reminder of what you need to do, and there's nothing more gratifying than crossing off each task, assignment, or chore as you complete it.

Procrastination: Waiting until the last minute to work on a long-term project is a guaranteed way to make your life stressful. Instead of scrambling around to finish a project that you've known about for months, break the job down into mini assignments that you can complete every night. On a calendar, count the days backward from the due date to figure out how soon you need to start working.

Help: It's a word—not a sign of weakness. Whenever school becomes overwhelming or you feel like you can't keep up, ask for help. It's easy to get wrapped up in your own schedule, and sometimes it takes an outsider's insight to make you see the solution. Guidance counselors, teachers, and even your parents can offer advice and help you through tense times in your life.

parental PRESSURE

Up until now, Mom and Dad have been major influences in your life, and all the big decisions that affected your future—from where you went to school to what you did with your free time—were made by your parents. But as you get into your high school groove, the dynamic of your relationship with your parents will start to change. You'll start to make your own decisions based on your goals and realize that you can make wise choices without your parents' input. The more you grow and learn about yourself, the more independent you become and the more you break away from your parents' influence. This is the time that you should begin to establish yourself as a separate person, which doesn't mean that your parents' opinions don't matter or that you don't have to listen to them anymore. It simply means that you're growing into your new role as an individual and preparing yourself for the day when you—and only you—make decisions about your life.

This is all part of the growing-up process, but that doesn't mean it's an easy transition. For starters, your parents might have a hard time dealing with your new sense of independence. They've supported and guided you for so many years, it may be difficult for them to accept that you can make your own decisions. They may feel like they know you best and therefore know what's best for you. The reality is, what they want and what you want might be completely different.

Unfortunately, this can make for tense moments between you and your parents. Say you've always wanted to go to art school, but your parents have been saving for your college education for years—and they really want you to be pre-med. If you fight for your beliefs, your parents may feel like you're making a mistake or that you don't appreciate them. But if you cave in to their pressure and ignore your own desires, you might resent your parents or regret not following your instincts. It seems like a lose-lose situation, but there is a middle ground in this battlefield.

At some point your parents have to realize that you need to make your own mistakes and celebrate your own successes in order to grow. At the same time, you have to understand that your parents sometimes do know best. They've lived and learned the same lessons, and their advice can be invaluable when you're making decisions. So, when it seems like World War III is about to break out in your household, remember these bits of advice on how to stand your ground (and when to give in):

- Tune in to your dreams. Figure out what makes you happy and what your interests are. Whether it's painting or politics, take the time to develop your talents. This sends a loud-and-clear message to your parents that your passion isn't a passing phase.

- Talk to your parents. Although you don't have to let them in on every last detail of your life, you should feel comfortable talking to them about your goals, your future, and your interests. Sure, your goals might change every other day, but chatting with your parents about this stuff lets them know that you value their opinions and need their support.

- Don't argue; discuss. If your parents disagree with a decision or don't understand your goals, talk to them the same way you'd talk to a friend—openly, honestly, and without anger or resentment. Make it clear to them why you think your decision is right for you. When talking turns into a screaming session, you're only proving your parents right. If you're not mature enough to handle a calm conversation about your future, you're not prepared for the future.

- Make your future yours. Don't buy in to your parents' plans just because you don't want to hurt their feelings or because you're afraid to speak your mind. If you follow their lead to make them happy, you'll only make yourself miserable.

- Agree to disagree. If your parents' plans don't jibe with your goals, be sure they know that you're not rejecting them. You don't have to put down their ideas or even convince them that they're wrong. You simply have to make a case for yourself. Be a good diplomat and explain how you realized your goals, what you hope to get out of achieving those goals, and how you plan to reach those goals.

- Compromise. Maybe there's room in your life for your goals and your parents' grand plans. If you can negotiate a plan of action that suits your style and makes your parents happy at the same time, go for it!

Chapter 6

the ins
AND OUTS
OF THE HIGH SCHOOL SOCIAL SCENE

Between the freaks and geeks, jocks and cheerleaders, burnouts and brains, trying to fit in with the right crowd can be harder than all of your classes combined. Whether you like it or not, cliques are a way of life in most high schools, and they can make life miserable for people who are struggling to

fit in. But finding your niche in school

doesn't mean you have to sacrifice your

identity. Just as your classes are teach-

ing you to be an independent learner,

navigating the social scene can teach you

how to be an independent person with dif-

ferent ideas, beliefs, and interests.

R-e-s-p-e-c-t

your fellow STUDENTS

High school is like a mini version of the outside world. Classrooms are filled with people with different backgrounds and beliefs—from race to religion to financial status. In a perfect world, people would accept and celebrate those differences for what they teach us about each other. Unfortunately, many people think that being different means you're "weird" or just plain "wrong." The truth is, when it comes to people, there is no right or wrong. You might disagree with someone, or you might not like the way some people live their lives, but we're all on this planet together and we have to learn to accept those differences.

Ironically, although high school is the place where you're supposed to learn and grow into an adult, it's also the place where some students perfect the art of schoolyard bullying. Calling someone names, bad-mouthing a fellow student, or trying to intimidate someone who is different in any way is wrong, no matter how you look at it. In middle school it was called "teasing," and everyone chalked it up to immaturity. In high school it's called "discrimination" and "harassment," more serious offenses that aren't so easily dismissed.

The Tolerance Test

Put your beliefs to the test. Check out these frequently asked questions to find out if your attitude about others makes the grade.

What's the difference between prejudice, discrimination, and harassment?

Prejudice means having preconceived ideas (usually negative) about a person or group of people based on skin color, sex, religion, sexual orientation, or any other difference.

Example: All rich people are snobby, rude, and self-absorbed.

Discrimination is the act of showing partiality or prejudice, which means you treat someone differently based on your prejudice.

Example: Because I think rich people are snobby, rude, and self-absorbed, I won't let a rich kid join a club that I started.

Harassment means physically or verbally attacking someone because of his or her differences and your prejudice.

Example: I called Sheila a stuck-up witch and pushed her into a locker because she thinks she's so much better than me.

What if I'm just teasing someone, and they think I'm harassing them?

It's not how you dish it—it's how the other person takes it. You might think you're joking around with someone, but maybe he or she is afraid of you or thinks you're being serious. It doesn't matter if you were "just kidding"—if the person you're "teasing" takes you seriously, you are guilty of harassment.

What should I do if someone is discriminating against me or harassing me?

First, try confronting the person who's harassing you. He or she may not realize that you're hurt, so explain how you feel and ask the person to stop. Sometimes speaking up for yourself is enough to put an end to the abuse. Whatever you do, don't play the same game and insult or harass the person who's harassing you. That will only provoke him or her and may make the situation worse. If confronting the person doesn't help, tell a teacher, a counselor at your school, your parents, or any adult you trust. Suffering in silence will not make the problem go away. In fact, the more you put up with someone hurting you, the worse it might get. By keeping quiet, you're telling that person that he or she can get away with harassing you.

How can I make sure I'm not being prejudiced or discriminating against someone?

For starters, realize that the things that make people different—skin color, beliefs, ethnic background, gender, sexual preferences, language, body shapes, and physical abilities—are what make people unique. As cliché as it sounds, variety is the spice of life. If everyone at your school looked alike and shared the same beliefs, life would be boring. Instead of dismissing people for being different, get to know them. You might accidentally learn something new or, better yet, see life from someone else's perspective. Besides, disliking someone or, worse, intentionally hurting someone simply for being who he or she is is like spanking a dog for wagging its tail.

friend or FAUX?

When classes have you going crazy and life itself is a little bit loony, your true friends are the people who will make your life more sane. Surrounding yourself with supportive, reliable friends is one of the most important things you can do for yourself in high school.

Unfortunately, whether you've been soul mates since kindergarten or you meet new people to pal around with, friendships change. As you get older and realize what's important to you, you may lose touch with—or outgrow—friends you've known for years. By the same token, even some of your new friends will come and go. The most important thing to remember is to stay true to yourself and stick with friends who make you a better person—not people who can make you popular.

Friends to Choose: People Who . . .

aren't afraid to tell you when you're screwing up or help you when you're down and out; share your interests and make you feel good about yourself; won't judge you; have seen you at your best and your worst and treat you the same no matter what you look, feel, or act like; you can trust with your deepest, darkest secrets.

Friends to Lose: People Who . . .

say one thing to your face and another thing behind your back; disappear when you need them most; put you or your other friends down; have only seen one side of your personality; betray your trust; are nice to you one day, then dump you the next; make you feel insecure or ashamed of yourself; don't understand your passions or dreams.

Friend vs. Friend

Even the best of friends have blowouts every now and then. But it shouldn't take a Supreme Court hearing to settle a dispute. If you have a fight with your friend, simply LEAP.

Listen to your friend's side of the story.

Explain your side of the story.

Apologize (and mean it!).

Push on—don't dwell on the past.

DATING
and
RELATING

Life was easy when you were five. Merely looking at a member of the opposite sex was grounds for a cootie shot, and you never had to worry about being smooth or having good breath. But times change, and all of a sudden dating is a big deal. The fact is, people develop at different paces, and you might be years away from finding the person of your dreams. In the meantime high school is a great time to scope out the scene and figure out what you want in a relationship. But remember: No one ever said romance was easy. Check out these dating dilemmas.

Why don't I have a boyfriend/girlfriend?

Despite how you might feel right now, the answer is not, "Because you're a two-headed beast and no one likes you." Chances are, either you haven't found the right person or you're too chicken to ask anyone out. If you're waiting for Ms./Mr. Right, great! Finding the right person is like searching for the right pair of shoes. You might encounter the most stylish, fabulous pair in the world, but the shoe still needs to fit in order to be comfortable. If you're suffering from the poultry syndrome, get a grip. You can't wait around for someone to ask you out, and you can't spend your life in fear of rejection. Yes, you will get turned down. Is it the end of the world? Uh, no.

What should I do if I have feelings for my best friend?

This is a little trickier than walking up to a stranger because you run the risk of losing a friend if the relationship doesn't last or making things "weird" if your friend doesn't share your feelings. You have two choices: You can tell your friend how you feel and leave the ball in his/her court, or you can bury your emotions and turn into a basket case every time he/she is around. In either case, your friend is going to find out how you feel by your actions. You can also think about it this way. You're friends with this person for a reason: You share similar interests, you're comfortable around each other, you help each other, and you probably make each other laugh. Those are all qualities you want in a romantic relationship, so you have more to lose if you don't say anything.

What are some signs of a relationship that's gone sour?

It's definitely time to hit the road when the person you're with is (1) abusive (physically or verbally) or (2) into the relationship more or less than you are. In both of these situations, the relationship is off balance. A healthy relationship is based on honesty, trust, and equality—if one person has all the control or power in a relationship, the other person is merely a pawn.

My significant other is extremely jealous. Should I be flattered or afraid?

Most likely afraid. When a boyfriend/girlfriend needs to know where you are and who you're with all the time, or tells you how to dress, or freaks when you even speak to a member of the opposite sex, there's a problem. The person you're with is insecure, and trying to control your every move is his/her way of making sure you don't find someone "better." Lots of times this kind of jealousy is just the beginning of an abusive relationship. It is better to get out of the relationship before it gets worse.

How can I break up with someone without hurting his/her feelings?

The truth is, you can't (unless the other person really didn't like you in the first place, and even then, dumping them will damage their ego). Breakups aren't easy, but that doesn't mean you should stay in a dead-end relationship to avoid a confrontation. The most important thing to remember is this: Be honest. If there's no chance you'll ever date this person again, make a clean break and don't leave the door open. If you even hint that there's a chance of reuniting, the other person will cling to that hope and never move on. As much as you'd like to "just be friends," it will take the other person a little while to get over the breakup, so give him/her some space.

How do I deal if I get dumped?

Just like the old saying goes, "Time heals all wounds." There's no quick, easy fix for a broken heart after a breakup—you just need time to get over it. The worst thing you can do is dwell on getting dumped instead of moving on with your life. The best thing you can do is get involved in other activities that take your mind off the breakup, like taking on more responsibilities in a club you belong to, making more time for your hobbies and interests, or volunteering. The more active you are, the more you'll realize that your life does have meaning without your ex.

Why are my friends mad at me for having a boyfriend/girlfriend?

Chances are, your boyfriend/girlfriend is now the center of your universe, and you've been neglecting those friends who have been with you through thick and thin. It happens all the time. You get so wrapped up in being part of a couple that you sideline the other things that gave your life meaning, including your friends. Relationships shouldn't interfere with the life you had before you were "attached"—they should complement it. Balance is key. You should be able to maintain your own identity within the relationship as well as your friendships, goals, and interests outside of the relationship. It might take a little effort on your part, but you have to make time for your friends and keep up with the life you had before you were in a relationship.

How do you know when you're ready for sex?

A good rule of thumb is this: If you're not sure, you're probably not ready. Sex is not a natural conclusion to every relationship, and it's definitely not something you want to rush into. There are risks that go hand in hand with sex, like unplanned pregnancies and sexually transmitted diseases, and before you subject yourself to those risks, you should answer a few questions about this big decision. For starters, why do you want to have sex? Is it because your partner is pressuring you or you think he/she will dump you if you don't? Also, are you completely comfortable with your partner, and can you talk openly with him/her about your relationship and sex? Do you trust your significant other? Have you talked about safe sex options? How do you think sex will change the relationship? These are just a few questions you and your partner should answer together before you even think about doing the deed. If you can't discuss these questions with him/her, you are definitely not ready to have sex.

getting along with GROWN-UPS

Now that you're dealing with everything from sex and school to careers and college, you probably feel more like an adult than ever before, but that doesn't mean you are an adult. You still have to respect the rules and authority of real adults (think teachers, parents, etc.) because, like it or not, you have a lot to learn from these people. At the same time you have to start asserting yourself as a responsible, reasonable individual who deserves the same respect. Here are a few ground rules for handling grown-ups when you're trying to stand up for yourself.

- Act like an adult if you want to be treated like an adult. That means no tantrums or holding your breath until you're blue in the face. Don't curse, scream, or lose your cool. Being polite, well-spoken, and calm can be a big factor in how your argument is received.

- Think before you speak. Write down the points you want to make, think about the pros and cons of your argument, and answer any questions you might be asked before you start this conversation. Your preparation will pay off.

- Don't expect an immediate answer. Although you're prepared for the conversation, the person you're talking to is not. Cornering someone on the spot can put him or her on the defensive, so make your point and back off. You need to give the other person time to think.

- Be willing to compromise. You might not get your way one hundred percent of the time, but adults are reasonable people. If you make a convincing case for yourself, they might be willing to meet you halfway.

- Listen and learn. You're not the only person with a point to make, so pay adults the same respect they give you—listen to what they have to say, then discuss it. Don't interrupt or jump to conclusions before you've heard their side.

- Don't be a sore loser. Pouting and whining will get you nowhere. Even if you "lose" your argument, you'll lose even more (think respect, dignity) if you resort to sulking.

ANGER

management 101

It's a fact of life: Stuff happens. Maybe you flunked a test, or your teacher embarrassed you in front of the class. Maybe you're dealing with a bad breakup or a family crisis. Everyone has bad days, but you can't blow your cool in the heat of the moment. It's okay to feel angry or upset, and venting your feelings will help you feel better, but you have to learn healthy ways to let your feelings flow. Note: Punching walls and screaming at your family is not healthy.

When You Need To Blow Off Some Steam

•Express yourself . . . on paper. Let all your emotions out in your journal, or write a letter to the object of your anger and tear it into pieces when you're done.

•Exercise. A long walk, a hard run, or twenty minutes on a treadmill will not only calm your nerves, it will also give you time to think about your next move.

•Talk to someone. Confide in a friend or an adult whom you trust about what's bothering you. Sometimes just talking about your problems can make them seem less, well, problematic.

•Find a quiet, isolated place and have a meltdown. Letting yourself cry or scream in a "safe" zone will neutralize your anger.

The Rules of Conflict Resolution

1. Use "I feel" statements rather than accusations.

2. Speak honestly and specifically about what you are angry about.

3. Allow each party involved to speak uninterrupted.

4. Allow each party involved to describe their best-possible outcome.

5. Try to reach a compromise.

QUIZ:
Do you stand up for yourself?

Find out if you speak your mind when it comes to making decisions.

Answer true or false for the following questions:

1. Despite your objections, your best friend swiped a copy of the history final. It's your weakest subject, though, and acing the exam would really help your final grade in the class. You:
a) take a peek at it. Why waste a good resource, right?
b) refuse to use the test and tell your friend that cheating is unfair to the rest of the class.

2. One of your friends tells an offensive joke that pokes fun at handicapped people—he or she apparently forgot that you're a Special Olympics volunteer. Everyone else is laughing, so you:
a) suck it up and don't say a word. There's no need to make a bad situation worse by confronting the comedian.
b) say, "Hey, if you're ever interested in helping out with the Special Olympics, they could use more volunteers with a sense of humor."

3. A kid in the cool crowd asks if you'll "be a pal" and lend him money, even though he's never so much as noticed you before now. You:
a) cough up the cash—this could be your big shot at hanging with the popular people.
b) politely decline, saying you just blew your allowance on the new Beck CD.

4. You're the most dependable person on the team, and the coach always asks you to stay late after practice to sort and put away the equipment. But after a while being the team's picker-upper is starting to grate on your nerves. You:

a) keep up the good work, hoping the coach sees your extra efforts and lets you off the hook one of these days.

b) recommend a rotating schedule so that a different team member is doing post-practice duty every day.

5. There's a tough geometry test tomorrow, but just as you settle in to start studying, your friend calls and is crying on the phone over a relationship—the third one this month. You:

a) drop your books and run to the rescue. Friends in need are way more important than some dumb test.

b) give yourself 15 minutes on the phone to counsel and console your heartbroken friend, then get back to studying.

Scoring:

If you chose mostly As

YOU'RE A DOOMED DOORMAT. That footprint on your head didn't get there by accident. Whenever you have to choose between doing what you know is right and giving in to what other people want, you always opt for making other people happy at your own expense. Giving in might be the path of least resistance, but never saying no or expressing your opinion isn't the way to win friends. Ultimately, being the go-to-guy or girl is going to get old, and you'll start to resent it. Try standing up for yourself, even if it means disappointing a friend. You'll feel a little more in control of your life.

If you chose mostly Bs

YOU'RE A STAND-UP STUDENT. You have no trouble saying what's on your mind or asserting yourself when someone's trying to take advantage of your good nature. Listening to your gut instinct is a good way to judge whether giving in or going your own way is the best thing to do, and you've got that skill down to a science—keep up the good work!

Chapter 7

now WHAT?

LIFE AFTER HIGH SCHOOL

ow that you've conquered high

school, are you ready for what's next?

Life after high school can seem daunting, but with that diploma in hand, your

possibilities are endless. Read on for

more about what your future may hold.

BACK

to school

Going off to college after you graduate isn't as simple as it sounds because there's more than one type of school to choose from. Here's how it breaks down:

COLLEGE
vs.
university

Technically, a university is bigger than a college, and it usually includes many different undergraduate and graduate schools. For example, a university might have a medical school, a business school, and a law school in addition to its undergraduate school. Classes at a university or a four-year professional college are usually focused on practical majors, like engineering, nursing, or business, which prepare you for a career.

Colleges, in the traditional sense, tend to be smaller schools that offer a liberal arts education—in other words, you take classes that give you a broad range of knowledge in subjects like art, history, psychology, and political science instead of focused, career-specific classes.

Two-year community colleges (aka junior colleges) admit anyone who has a high school diploma (or the equivalent). If your grades in high school weren't hot enough to get you into a four-year college or if you want to test the waters without paying big bucks for an expensive school, junior colleges are the way to go. If you complete a two-year program and get an associate's degree, you have the option of transferring into a four-year college to complete the last two years of your degree.

Technical institutes or trade schools are privately owned schools that offer hands-on job training in all sorts of trades, from computers to auto mechanics to fashion design to medical assistance. The classes are geared toward specific careers, and most schools have job placement resources that will get you out of the classroom and into a job as soon as you graduate.

QUESTIONS to consider during YOUR COLLEGE HUNT

Do I want to live close to home or far away?

Do I want to attend a single-sex or co-ed school?

Do I want to live on campus or commute to school?

Do I want a specialized program or a wide variety of majors to choose from?

Do I want to go to a big university or a small college?

Do I want to go to college in the city, the suburbs, or a rural area?

Do I want to go to a big sports school?

Is cost a factor in choosing a school?

C●llege Checklist

Once you answer the questions on the facing page, you should have a better idea about what kind of college you're interested in attending. That's the easy part. Now you have to go through the process of applying to college, which takes time, concentration, and, yes, money. Here's a checklist of things you have to do in order to get into college.

By the End of Your Junior Year:

- Make a college binder, complete with paper, pockets, and a calendar with important deadlines and exam dates marked on it.
- Take the ACT, PSAT, SAT, and any other college entrance exams that might be required by the schools you're interested in attending.
- Research schools. Surf the Internet or browse a guide to colleges for information about schools that interest you.
- Make a list in your college binder of schools you want to go to. Give each school a separate page (or two) and write in the pros and cons of each school (think location, school size, tuition, etc.). Also, include information about entrance requirements (GPA, essays, SAT scores), addresses, important phone numbers, and other contact information.
- Visit as many of the schools on your list as possible.

At the Beginning of Your Senior Year:

- Narrow down your list of colleges by weeding out schools that you're not interested in anymore.
- Call your list of prospective schools and ask for applications.
- Write the deadline for each of your applications in your college binder calendar.
- Write the required essays for the applications.
- Gather your application materials, including application fee, transcripts, entrance exam scores, GPA, at least two letters of recommendation, and essay.
- Submit your applications before the deadline.
- Schedule a practice interview with your guidance counselor or college adviser.
- Schedule interviews with the admissions office at your prospective schools. If possible, arrange for campus tours and overnight stays where you're interviewing to get a better feel for campus life.
- Wait for all your acceptance letters to arrive!

SKIPPING school

If you don't get into the colleges on your hit list, or if you can't handle the thought of getting back into the school routine so soon after you graduate, check out these options:

Apprenticeships are the most traditional way to learn a craft, like wood-working and carpentry. Instead of spending time in a classroom, you work under the supervision of an experienced person who knows the craft. You get paid as an apprentice, and you get the benefit of hands-on training and real-world experience.

Military duty (think army, navy, air force, marines) also pays you while you get on-the-job training in technical fields. When you finish your tour of duty, you're entitled to financial assistance for college, or you can apply your experience to a civilian job. You could also attend a military college, like West Point. Acceptance into these schools requires tremendous mental and physical abilities, but tuition is free. If you choose to go to a non-military college after high school, you can apply for an ROTC (Reserve Officer Training Corps) scholarship. During college, you'll spend one weekend a month training, and after you graduate, you're required to serve in the military.

Taking time off from school is a viable option, but only if you've eliminated your other options with good reasons. This doesn't give you license to hang out and do nothing—if you take time off, you're supposed to use that time to prepare for when you "return," whether you want to go back to school or get a job. You should plan to spend the year getting involved in activities or interests that might help you clarify your goals and get you back on track. Your plan of action might include the following:

Thirteenth-year studies are offered at many private boarding schools to students who need help with their academic standing. The senior-plus year gives students a chance to bring up grades and SAT scores, which means they'll have a better shot at getting into college.

Traveling abroad is an eye-opening experience for anyone who's not ready to go to college but still wants an education in the ways of the world.

Working at a full-time job during your time-off year will give you a taste of reality. It may also help you decide what you want to do with your life, whether you discover a career path or decide that college is the place for you.

Volunteering is a great opportunity for civic-minded graduates who want to give something back to the world. Working with others and lending a helping hand will give you a sense of purpose and accomplishment while you decide what you want to do.

QUIZ:
Are You a Doer
or a Downer?

Find out if you've got what it takes to make things happen—
in your life, at school, and at home.

1. The environmental club is looking for members to volunteer for a sit-in at a local park to protest proposed plans to cut down a 100-year-old tree. You:
a) suddenly get the urge to tie your shoelaces—thus ducking below the volunteer radar—and think, Let the enviro-troopers come to the rescue.
b) add your name to the list, only after your friends guilt trip you into volunteering.
c) are the first one with your hand waving in the air. After all, if you don't stand up for the tree's rights, who will?

2. When it's your turn to do the dishes after dinner, you:
a) wait until the food is fossilized on the plates. You've got better things to do, like watch TV.
b) are a big believer in the philosophy "a little goes a long way," so you let 'em soak until they're clean.
c) get it over with ASAP so you can get on with the rest of your life.

3. You're dying to ask your crush to the Homecoming dance, but you're terrified of rejection. You:
a) boycott the dance altogether—who needs the stress?
b) decide to ask your crush, but only if your backup date says no first.
c) plot a one-of-a-kind dance proposal that will make your crush notice you, regardless of whether she says yes or no.

4. The school dress code is as outdated as poodle skirts and wing tips, but most people seem content with just complaining about it. You, on the other hand:
a) are constantly getting written up and sent home for breaking the dress code.
b) have no problems sticking to the status quo—it beats getting into a confrontation with the school principal any day.
c) have been circulating a petition and researching the way to get school codes changed.

5. When you send your high school transcript to the colleges of your choice:

a) they'll see your GPA and lots of white space.

b) It'll be filled with clubs you joined for the sole purpose of impressing college admissions officers.

c) they'll need extra pages to fit all of your extracurricular activities and honors you earned.

Scoring:

If you chose mostly As
BARELY BREATHING

On the Richter scale of activity, you'd register way below zero. It's not that you can't get motivated and excited about your life—it's that you *won't*. Maybe you're afraid of failing, or worried that friends will hassle you about getting actively involved—but the fact of the matter is you're only short-changing yourself. The solution? Get out there! Push yourself to do different things, hang with new people, or join a club that interests you. A little effort can make all the difference.

If you chose mostly Bs
MASTER OF THE BARE MINIMUM

When push comes to shove, you'll get the job done...barely. Your MO is doing just enough to get by but never fully committing yourself to a project or a goal. But there's hope for you yet. Discipline yourself and start doing things 110 percent. Don't just volunteer for a cleanup crew, appoint yourself trash team leader. Instead of joining clubs for résumé filler, start your own special-interest organizations. Once you succeed, you'll see that a job well done is a better reward than scraping by on the bare minimum.

If you chose mostly Cs
ALL THE WAY WORKER

Take your right hand, reach over your left shoulder and give yourself a nice pat on the back. You've got "natural born leader" written all over your future because you throw yourself into your work 100 percent, without fear of failure or embarrassment. When there's a job to do, people instinctively turn to you for help because you never let them down. And, on those rare occasions when a plan flops, you're not one to wallow in self-pity—you're already on to the next challenge!

c●nclusi●n

So there you have it: everything you need to know about high school and more. The truth is, the next four years of your life will be full of surprises. There will be heartbreak and stress, friendship dramas and impossible teachers, but you'll also experience your fair share of thrills, success, and happiness. No one ever said high school would be easy, but if you've made it this far, chances are you're ready to tackle anything that comes your way. Remember: You're one step closer to the daunting task of becoming a full-blown adult, but you're also smack-dab in the middle of the most carefree chapter of your life, so take advantage of it while you can. This is the time to explore, take risks, find yourself, and dare to believe in your own unlimited potential. There is no exact formula or set of rules for succeeding in high school, but if you're willing to work hard and you're prepared to face the challenges of your new world, you'll survive. You might even have fun while you're at it!